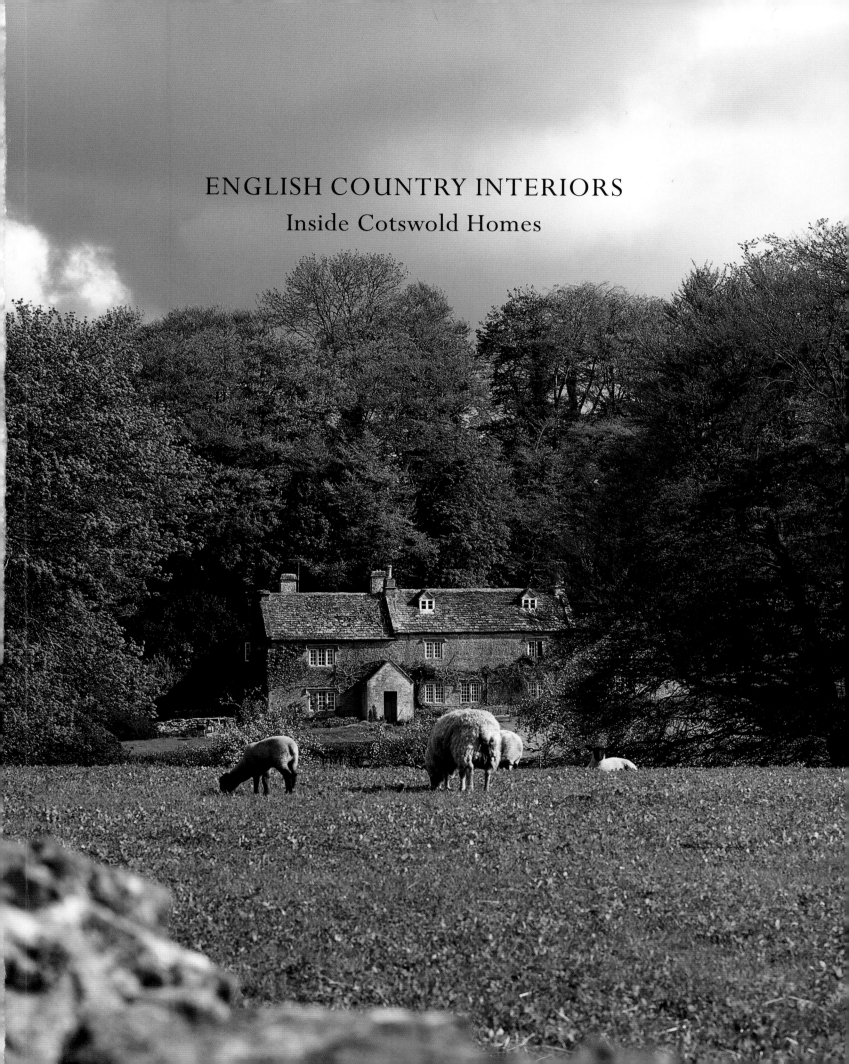

ENGLISH COUNTRY INTERIORS
Inside Cotswold Homes

ENGLISH COUNTRY INTERIORS
Inside Cotswold Homes

Sarah North

Photography by
Mark Nicholson

MITCHELL BEAZLEY

English Country Interiors

Inside Cotswold Homes

Idea conceived and compiled by
Mark Nicholson and Rachel Jones

First published in Great Britain in 2004 by Mitchell Beazley,
an imprint of Octopus Publishing Group Ltd,
2–4 Heron Quays, London, E14 4JP

Copyright © Octopus Publishing Group Ltd 2004
Photographs © Mark Nicholson www.marknicholson.com
Text © Octopus Publishing Group Ltd 2004

Location Research & Styling	Rachel Jones
Senior Executive Editor	Anna Sanderson
Executive Art Editor	Auberon Hedgecoe
Senior Editor	Emily Anderson
Design	DW Design
Proofreader	Colette Campbell
Indexer	Helen Snaith
Production	Gary Hayes

ISBN 1 84000 866 0

A CIP record for this book is available
from the British Library

Set in Fairfield LH, Perpetua, and Univers
Produced by Toppan Printing Co., (HK) Ltd.
Printed and bound in China

To order this book as a gift or an incentive contact
Mitchell Beazley on 020 7531 8481

Contents

A Brief History of the Cotswolds

In the heart of England, amid well-wooded valleys and streams, the villages and towns are built from the same mellow, honey-coloured limestone that forms the hills around them. Churches of unexpected richness and grandeur sit alongside comfortable manor houses; golden almshouses and cottages huddle around undulating village greens and stone river bridges. This is the Cotswolds, where for centuries man and nature have worked in harmony to create one of the most aesthetically beautiful landscapes in England.

The origins of the name are Anglo Saxon, referring perhaps either to the sixth-century Saxon princeling, Cod, who owned a "wold" or forest here, or to the sheep "cots" or pens that covered these hills. What and where the Cotswolds are is more difficult to define. Some say they start at the Roman city of Bath in the south and run north-west to the medieval wool town of Chipping Campden, with Shakespeare's Avon Vale to the north. From Cleeve Hill, the Cotswolds' highest point, Wales can be seen on a clear day across the Severn vale. Evocatively named streams – the Windrush, Coln, Churn, and Leach – branch and wind their way through pretty, compact villages to join the Thames on its way to London. To the

west, thickly wooded valleys have been forged by the Rivers Frome and Isbourne and their tributaries, en route to the Rivers Severn and Avon. The north Cotswolds, from Northleach to Chipping Campden, feature rolling countryside comprising a series of dry valleys – clear evidence of Ice Age glacial activity. Clues as to the whereabouts and physical features of villages are often contained in their names: in the north, Cotswolds villages such as Cold Aston, Stow-on-the-Wold (around which, as folklore warns "the cold wind blows"), and Clapton-on-the-Hill accurately suggest exposed, hilltop sites. Conversely, Lower Slaughter, Morton-in-the-Marsh, Temple Guiting, and Bourton-on-the-Water elicit images of snug, sheltered positions.

Topographically the Cotswolds is 1,550km² (600 sq miles) of oolitic limestone belt, laid down 180 million years ago during the "Jurassic" demise of the dinosaurs. It is a stone particularly rich in fossils and easily worked when newly quarried, or "green", but, unlike chalk, it becomes stronger and more durable with age. When freshly quarried the stone is cream coloured, turning varying shades of buff, honey, and rust, depending on its mineral and iron content. Typically the colours of the stone are golden in the Bath area, honey-coloured around Broadway and Burford, and greyer in the Painswick area. In common to all regions is the stone's magical quality of retaining the light.

above Looking west across the village green at Little Barrington, December sunshine lights the golden faces of farmhouses and cottages above the brook.

left A row of houses in Sheep Street, Burford. Known sometimes as the "gateway" to the Cotswolds, Burford's prosperity over the centuries has relied on sheep, quarrying, and coaching.

overleaf A tall church spire, its outline blurred by the early morning mist, forms a typical backdrop to a Cotswold scene, where agricultural land and grazing animals encircle villages of honeyed limestone.

above Sheep have been
grazing in the Cotswolds
since pre-Roman times.
Cotswold fields are often
divided by the distinctive
dry-stone walls formed
by farmers picking
freestone from their fields.

Quarried stone was a good workable and exportable commodity, but it was not the
Cotswolds' only trump card. During the Middle Ages the area became the centre of
the English wool trade. Within Europe English wool was considered supreme, and
Cotswold wool was known to be the finest in England. Sheep have been grazing in
the Cotswolds since pre-Roman times, and by the thirteenth century there were around
500,000 sheep grazing in the region. Most wool was produced by the local breed, the
Cotswold Lion – a broad-backed animal with a distinctive "lovelock" falling over its face
and a mane-like fleece of long fibres. It was not possible in the Middle Ages to spin worsted
yarn from short-fibred wool so the long-stapled variety was in great demand, and the export
of Cotswold fleeces to Europe became a major contributor to the English economy.

The distinctive Cotswold architectural style evolved from the beautifully adorned, high-quality
masonry of the local church architecture, with its elaborate porches (such as on St John
the Baptist, Burford), ornamental parapets (St Mary's, Fairford), and hooded moulds over the
windows – a particular feature of Cotswold architecture. At the dissolution of the monasteries
under Henry VIII in the 1530s, vast church estates were transferred to favoured laymen,
former religious houses became privately owned, and recently acquired fortunes were

directed to creating new buildings or embellishing existing ones. The teams of masons who had hitherto laboured for abbot and priest now worked for successful wool merchants, and from the sixteenth century the Cotswold style developed around domestic architecture.

Its legacy is the wealth of stone dwellings ranging hierarchically from grandiose manor to yeoman farm, cottage, and almshouse. At the upper end of the scale, the medieval style of living in public with little privacy was giving way to a desire for more sophistication and comfort. Great halls increasingly were used only for ceremonial occasions, if retained at all, and new houses were built to include more private rooms for the family. Houses became bigger as more wings were added, but were still governed structurally by the materials they were built from, in particular the stone roof tiles. To prevent rain seeping between uneven joints in the roof, roof angles had to be steeper, resulting in tall, narrow, heavy roofs often requiring extra structural support from buttressed stone walls. To overcome wasted roof space, masons designed the characteristic Cotswold gable running along the length of the house, which enabled windows to be inserted into the roof. The excommunication of Henry VIII delayed the arrival in Britain of Renaissance influence for about a century, and during this period the Tudor style of architecture reached near perfection in the

above St. Oswald's, Widford, is known as the "church in the fields". Allegedly it stands on the site of the burial place of St. Oswald, who died here on his way to Gloucester from Lindisfarne.

Cotswolds. Locally quarried "freestone" served perfectly such Tudor mannerisms as mullioned windows, finials, four-centred arched doorways, drip moulds, string courses, and ecclesiastical hooded mouldings.

The Cotswolds today are easily accessible from all parts of southern England and, as they are only an hour-and-a-half from London, allow at least part-time commuting. Nevertheless, a significant proportion of the population work locally or from home, and traditional occupations still thrive in the area. Modern computer technology and better roads mean that, realistically, fast-lane businesses can be run from homes within unspoilt Cotswold villages still characterized by medieval church towers, ancient pubs, and clear streams. This new influx of people provides extra work for garden designers, architects, carpenters, and antiques dealers. And within the market towns and secluded settlements others who live and work in the Cotswolds find inspiration for solitary, creative occupations, such as writing, painting, sculpting, cooking, or interior design. A significant proportion still work directly with nature, farming the land or pursuing careers in equestrianism.

The Cotswolds remain largely unchanged. The towns and villages have grown, the pace of life is a little faster, but for centuries man has depended directly and indirectly on the landscape for his livelihood, and this is much the same today.

left A summer view across fields of corn to the village of Snowshill; houses with steeply gabled roofs squat in various stages of elevation against the ancient hillside.

below In the Spring black-faced lambs are an ubiquitous feature of Cotswold lowland farms. This one's black features are inherited from a Suffolk Ram.

overleaf A broad swathe of sunlit grass bisects a wood of beech trees. Spring sunlight filters through the dappled canopy of young beech leaves onto a purple carpet of bluebells.

The Cook
and the Converted Barn

The cook's passion for food started early and cooking has dictated the pattern of her life. Today she cooks for pleasure, to entertain family and friends in her "sunshine" barn of mellow Cotswold stone.

left A large stone fireplace, made by a local Cotswold company, is positioned centrally below the barn's original arrow slit windows to form an essential focus for the room. The large fire grate was also purpose-made.

right The central circular oak chopping board, designed and made by the cook's brother, was inspired by the kitchen table at Castle Drogo in Devon.

below The intrinsic ingredients of the cook's recipes are Mediterranean: peppers, tomatoes, herbs, garlic, and varied olive oils. Baskets of produce from the garden ripen on windowsills.

Great Rissington, Little Rissington, and Wyck Rissington lie southeast of Bourton-on-the-Water, within the beautiful Windrush valley. Eight years ago a cook with a passion both for the Cotswolds and for renovating old properties discovered a glorious south-facing site between the Rissingtons, with open, far-reaching views across the Barrington Estate. Comprising a cottage, large barn, and series of dog kennels, the plan to unite all three buildings into one house represented a challenge even for a family used to living among builders – this was their fourth move within the Cotswolds in 21 years. The cook is apparently someone who thrives on projects: an inexhaustible creative energy manifests itself in three main directions – interiors, entertaining, and silk flower arrangements – and the current house reflects a deep-rooted flair for all three.

The original cottage possessed charm and character, even in its dilapidated state, but a porch was added and arched Gothic mullioned windows replaced throughout. Internal doors either were removed completely to retain an open feel, or substituted by partially glazed ones found in local reclamation yards. Now the boundaries of barn and cottage have merged into one spectacular space where kitchen, dining area, and drawing room form the arterial heart of the house.

Rich, tawny, earthy colours abound. Aubusson tapestries hang from tall barn walls and antique textiles have been thrown across sofas, or remnants made into cushion covers. Bare

right In the main, south-facing bedroom the four-poster bed is adorned with rich, russet-coloured antique French textiles; the sofa at the foot of the bed was a local auction discovery. In the bathroom a large, gilt oval mirror sits above the bath.

córners have been filled with large, silk-flower displays. Solid timber beams and a two-hundred year-old oak floor create an organic, natural sense of space complemented by natural textures; wicker baskets are a predominant feature and the kitchen chairs' seats are made by a local craftsman specializing in baskets for balloons. Elsewhere there are ingenious touches of fund-saving compromise: an arch-topped wooden garden gate forms one end of a run of units; a sawn branch from a tree is the supporting limb to a work surface; and a pair of antique French doors have been modified to form the fronts of the kitchen cabinets.

In an area of the kitchen previously serving as the milking parlour, a desire to create an "evolved" rather than "fitted" look led to local countryside searches. An old, cast-iron butcher's meat rack now serves as a hanging rack for the copper pans she prefers to cook with. The painted green cabinet was found in Chipping Norton and antique French textile attached inside its bare door frames to hide the cooking cutters, bread, and flan tins kept there. A French marble-topped patisserie table was also collected locally.

From the kitchen tall barn doors lead to a gravel garden, formally and evenly partitioned by low box hedges. Nearly everything growing in this part of the garden is edible: bay

right In a corner of the kitchen that was the old dairy parlour, a French marble-topped patisserie table stands before a gothic south-facing window.

below left A view into the hall shows a fireplace formed from pillars from either side of an old Cotswold gateway, topped with a stone lintel. The glass hall doors were found in a reclamation yard.

22

trees stand on sentry duty either side of the doors, and in the summer a vine bearing sweet, strawberry-flavoured grapes extends from the terrace to an upstairs south-facing balcony constructed from an old oak manger salvaged from a Cotswold reclamation yard. Herbs of every description grow profusely in the garden and espalier fruit trees have been trained along the west-facing walls that once formed the boundary of the dog kennels.

The house throughout reflects the attention of a resourceful creator and collector. The space she has created is enriched by antique textiles and by unusual furniture "finds", ingeniously amalgamated to create a house designed to facilitate the cook's love and flair for entertaining friends and family on a grand scale.

below Tall barn doors lead to a walled gravel garden laid with box hedges and filled with edible plants – bay trees, strawberry-flavoured grapes, herbs, and fruit trees.

right Candlesticks adorn many surfaces. Cushions made from tapestry remnants reflect a love of antique textiles consistently displayed throughout the house.

The Artist

and the Mill

The artist is inspired by her home surroundings, a stone-built water mill on the River Leach where it emerges from the Cotswold uplands and follows its course through flat fields to join the Thames.

left Antique wooden bedroom furniture has been cleverly arranged to fit uncompromising ceiling angles; a beam bisects the original gothic window, estimated to be around 400 years old.

right Inside the mill the ceilings are low, and straight, structural lines non-existent. The mellow, amber warmth of the tobacco-coloured wallpaper compliments the polished wooden floors and antique English furniture.

In the late-nineteenth century a journalist called Stanley Baron wrote in a local Cotswold newspaper: "I have just seen a sight to warm the hearts of all who love old England – a mill stream in full spate, a colonnade of full-grown beeches in all their autumn glory and a stone-built water mill still grinding corn on the same spot as in the days of Domesday Book ..."

It was in this mill, some 70 years later, that an artist and her husband made their home. No longer does water cascade from the mill wheel, nor does a cowbell linked with a strap above the millstones clang a warning that the grain supply is slowing, but the site remains delightfully unchanged and all the working components of the corn mill have been retained. In the late-nineteenth century the local estate used this mill as a showpiece. New machinery had been installed and grand weekend visitors would be brought to meet the miller and be shown the pulleys and belts, and series of "state-of-the-art" cog wheels that uniquely used yew wood and cast iron teeth alternately. The present incumbents have left all the machinery in place, viewing it as evocative of the best of solid Victorian engineering. It forms the dynamic if unusual backdrop for an art gallery where, in addition to a permanent collection, regular private exhibitions are held showcasing local artists.

The stone mill is encircled almost entirely by running water, separated by swathes of suede-textured lawn and stone terraces. In the summer a sturdy hammock attached to an

right The drawing room is a typical example of English country-house style – polished wooden floor, antique rugs, large, open log fireplace, fresh flowers, and faded chintz-covered sofas and curtains.

ancient weeping willow swings precariously close to the surface of the River Leach. From the artist's studio window a wide canvas Italian umbrella shading comfortable outdoor chairs does not obscure a clear view of the river as it meanders north towards the Thames. It is a frequent source of inspiration, not only to the artist herself but to other local art groups who find the setting idyllic. In a corner of her studio, strongly reminiscent of the school art room for its pungent smells of turps and oils, are pictures by favourite masters, such as Manet and Bonnet, and by Vermeer whom she particularly admires for his ability to create space and atmosphere within his paintings.

Back in the nineteenth century the miller's wife took daily swims in the mill pool, whatever the weather. The door she used leads directly outside from the drawing room. The artist does not follow her predecessor's bracing example, although during warm weather she walks downstream, where she has recently discovered a deep and secluded pool. But for the artist in the mill the ultimate pleasure is derived from painting alongside her artist son and being able to share both inspiration and frustration. As a like-minded person he is the perfect companion, and being with him provides an opportunity to exchange new ideas and thoughts on the world of art. The Cotswold landscape and its constantly

right A small room on the mill's ground floor is now the artist's studio. The river flows close by in this corner of the house, and in the winter the fast-flowing water provides a dramatic backdrop to the artist at her easel.

below A view of the artist's studio across lawns and terraces, where terracotta pots with sculpted spheres of box trees soften the steep angles of stone-slated roof and gabled dormer windows.

changing views throughout the seasons animates and informs all aspects of their work. Summer valleys and hillsides – brilliant greens and fluorescent yellows on account of the rapeseed in the fields – add vivid tones to their palettes; fields of flax or linseed instigate cooler shades of blue.

The artist is modest about her own artistic flair; a course of lessons with an inspirational tutor re-ignited a great passion that had lain dormant since school. She is also inspired by an Italian artist, Morandi, who lived in Bologna and spent a lifetime painting small pots and bottles in his studio. His love of nature and the harmony he created in his paintings with the objects around him are a constant source of joy to the artist, who similarly aspires to capture the beauty of the humble items and shapes that surround her in the Cotswold landscape.

The Seamstress
and the Cottage

A two-hundred-year-old, one-bedroomed, wool
merchant's cottage in the heart of Witney has been
home to a seamstress for the last 20 years. Visiting
the seamstress' cottage is a journey back in time.

The bustling market town of Witney is positioned on the south-east periphery of the Oxfordshire Cotswolds. Famous for its blankets, Witney's industry survived the collapse of the Cotswold woollen industry after the Industrial Revolution. Pubs still bear names such as "The Fleece", and it is not unusual for old cottages to have narrow passages running through or between them as the long corridors were used for spinning yarn. Down one such passage, between two-hundred-year-old listed wool merchants' dwellings, large letters etched into a glass front door spell "Ladies' Tailor". A seamstress has lived here for 20 years.

At the top of the house, up two flights of treacherously steep stairs, is an attic workshop bearing all the hallmarks of the seamstress' trade. Four sewing machines, including one she inherited from her mother who was also a dressmaker and tailoress, are squeezed into the tiny, skylighted space, alongside rolls of material, piles of the magazine *Interiors* (taken religiously since its maiden publication), and boxes of old dressmaking patterns. Descending the stairs the seamstress must negotiate her way perilously past many boxes of vintage shoes.

The original oak attic door leads into the seamstress' bedroom, the main window of which overlooks a large green. Inherited books and china sit on the windowsill, presided

right A row of pretend paper mugs, which caught the seamstress' eye in a Witney kitchen shop, hang above the doorway beneath shelves of her parents' wedding china.

below One entire wall of the seamstress' bedroom is hidden behind shelves of books – Bibles, prayer books, and the complete works of William Shakespeare.

over by a gilt cherub. The seamstress confesses to a lifelong love of angels and it is suddenly very obvious: chubby angelic images, mainly gilt ones, hover and flutter throughout the cottage.

Keeping and collecting old costumes is another overriding passion. The seamstress has framed her mother's wedding dress, worn in 1911. It hangs on a wall beside stairs leading up from the "front room" into the bedroom. With an eye trained for precision and detail, she draws attention to the tiny covered buckle on the belt, the metal loops bound exquisitely in stitched silk, and the demure, braided neckline.

Other memorabilia displayed downstairs include her father's christening robe, complete with cape, and a close friend's naval uniform with its traditional white piping that was stitched onto the navy collar by the seamen themselves. An all too-lifelike mannequin, complete with black wig wound into a bun, stands near the window. She is wearing an ivory silk wedding dress with stitched covered buttons and silk fringing. It was acquired from a charity shop in Witney but experts at the Bath Costume Museum put a valuable mid-nineteenth century date on it.

Born in Lancashire during the depression, and living through the deprivations of World War II, the seamstress has grown up with a deep-seated compulsion to keep everything, not only from her own life but also from her family's. In the kitchen an original external Cotswold stone wall is adorned with plates and other treasures from the past – her parents' wedding-day "loving cups", the clogs her grandfather made for workers in the mills, and even her father's razor. A thrift-shop queen, she continues to collect and still finds nooks and crannies to display her booty within the tiny one-bedroomed cottage.

above Two Steiff bears face the room. Their steel-rimmed spectacles belonged to the seamstress' grandmothers; one teddy bear wears the seamstress' old school tie.

right In the attic workshop a tailors' dummy wears a delicate, ivory lace dress of miniscule proportions, once worn on stage by the actress Phyllis Calvert.

The Bed & Breakfast

and the Old Vicarage

The quintessentially English bed-and-breakfast industry flourishes in the Cotswolds, where doors are opened to visitors, offering them the chance to become pampered guests in a fine country house.

In a small village in the Windrush valley a stone bridge spans the river and the lane is lined with both Cotswold stone-tiled and thatched roofed cottages. At the far end of the village, where the road narrows and rises a little, a lane leads to a fifteenth-century church and the romantic ruins of a fortified manor house. It also passes the Old Vicarage, which is featured regularly in reputable British guides to bed-and-breakfast establishments as: "Country elegance with few concessions to modernity. Rugs and furniture fit beautifully. The River Windrush trickles through the garden".

The picture wasn't as harmonious when the present owner bought the house at auction some 30 years ago. As was the case throughout England, the church was unable to sustain the maintenance costs of a large stone vicarage; there was no heating, meaning the vicar inhabited one room only, the garden was overgrown and the house had become dilapidated. Now, upstairs, walls have been removed to create a large landing with a glorious sense of sun and space, and the well-tended garden slopes to the river as it follows an S-shaped course

above The breakfast room is lit by overhead lights on a weighted pulley system, salvaged from a billiard room. A French *bergere* sofa sits beneath the large window.

right The four-poster bed was constructed around a standard divan bed. A French painted wardrobe decorated with cane is accompanied by a small cane chair.

left The bedposts are covered with pink moire silk and Indian material forms the back hanging. The exotic bedhead echoes the curves of the Taj Mahal, but the bedcover is quintessentially English, white, broderie anglaise linen.

below right The bathroom wallpaper is reminiscent of a colourful English meadow. A traditional brass showerhead is reflected in the tall, full-length mirror.

around the house. On the lawn copper beech, silver birch, lime, and sycamore trees cast dappled shade and, in the late spring, Queen Anne's lace (cow parsley) froths tall and wispy.

That the Old Vicarage is a living, breathing, family house, home to seven grown-up children, is evident throughout. At the foot of the steep, sisal-covered staircase is a collection of all the paraphernalia of their presence (tennis racquets, footballs, cricket bats, fishing rods, and assorted hats). The house displays an eclectic mix of furniture found in antique shops, and paintings gathered in England and abroad. Inconceivable to modern architects, six doors lead out of the hall (including those to the cellar, stairs, and garden) making it an ideal theatre in which the children, when younger, performed plays written by their father.

A dark, treacly smell, redolent of myriads of open log fires, pervades the study. Bookshelves
were built to accommodate the family's extensive book supply, now alphabetically ordered.
Textiles are gathered from numerous sources: an "old gold" brocade sofa has Indian silk
cushions; antique curtain tie-backs are French. In typically English country style the scent
from flowers freshly cut from the garden stimulates the senses throughout the house.

Upstairs, friends and bed-and-breakfasters receive the same four-star treatment. Four
double bedrooms and two bathrooms radiate off a central landing – previously a room with
narrow passages around its four walls. Bedrooms are characterized by their charming four-
postered beds, fresh white linen, and family photographs. Far from being fitted and
modern, the bathrooms are comfortable places to soak in deep, free-standing baths,
surrounded by framed needlework samplers and polished Edwardian cabinets displaying
collected china and glass.

Downstairs, in the kitchen, the Aga works overtime some mornings to produce cooked
English breakfasts, which, after a comfortable night's sleep in the Old Vicarage's serene
and elegant surroundings, fulfill all that's asked of the traditional British bed-and-breakfast.

The Beekeeper
and the Townhouse

The beekeeper lives in a Cotswold townhouse,
where collected bee paraphernalia reflects a lifelong
fascination with bees and the kitchen is central to
the process of extracting and bottling honey.

As Gloucestershire ends, the villages of honeyed limestone continue into Oxfordshire and the Thames valley. Within a Cotswold townhouse a beekeeper and his wife have made their home for the last 16 years. Now in his seventies, he developed a passion for honey bees as a child of six years old when, at his parent's home near Bideford, North Devon, he would frequently dodge his governess to seek the company of the head gardener who kept colonies of bees in a clearing overlooking the River Torridge. Although theoretically retired, he still keeps bees locally and helps others start out on this fascinating craft.

The beekeeper's current dwelling is a tall townhouse that rubs narrow, stone shoulders with its high-street neighbours on either side. On entering the white front door, attention is drawn immediately to the back of the house and to a kitchen and breakfast room bathed in natural overhead light. Beyond, French doors lead out into a charming, narrow cottage garden, at the foot of which is a fine metalwork arbour overgrown with clematis *tangutica* (Bill Mackenzie), alongside a thatched French beehive.

The kitchen itself is central not only to family life but also to the messy honey-production process that occurs twice a year in June and September. The beekeeper explains how, once the honey has been extracted from the hives, it is transferred into large buckets where it is warmed in the Aga's bottom oven before being filtered through muslin into a "ripener", which ensures that air bubbles rise to the surface before bottling.

Visitors to the house quickly become aware of the beekeeper's passion as the family collect bee paraphernalia and other objects from their travels abroad. On the dresser is an extensive collection of different china honey pots, gathered and given as presents by friends and family familiar with the beekeeper's lifelong hobby. On the kitchen table is a honeycomb butter dish around which china bees permanently hover and settle. Nearby,

left This bedroom is naturally well-lit by three windows overlooking the back garden. A passion for engravings is reflected in the pictures hanging on the pale blue walls.

below left In 1995 the beekeeper wrote an autobiographical book, *A Nomad Amongst the Bees*. Friend and artist Belinda Holland illustrated the front cover – the framed picture is her original painting.

right On the beekeeper's four-postered bed is an old American quilt, and on the wall hangs a picture, also American, of a beehive painted on velvet.

left In the garden a variegated *euonymous* has grown through an apple tree, casting dappled shade over the wrought-iron table and chairs. At the bottom of the garden nestles a thatched French beehive.

right To avoid being stung the beekeeper must wear protective clothing. A smoker simulates the effect of a forest fire, inducing the bees to engorge their honey sacs with honey and making them less likely to sting.

an ashtray bearing a colourful bee theme is a present from his daughter-in-law, as is a "beehive" plate and a mug decorated and painted by his grandchildren.

Upstairs, the dressing table beside the beekeeper's four-poster bed supports his collection of silver "honey show" medals, and an antique hygrometer for recording humidity – necessary to a beekeeper for estimating when the bees will deliver their main cargo of pollen and nectar. Needlework cushions on the bed with designs of hovering bees were created by a friend and by the beekeeper himself. In another bedroom the angled ceiling follows the lines of the steep roof – a characteristic feature of Cotswold houses. On the antique bedspread, against white linen pillows, favourite teddy bears – legacies from childhood – are unintentionally reminiscent of honey-fanatic Winnie-the-Pooh.

For the beekeeper the pleasure of beekeeping is not the end product but rather his fascination with the bee's lifecycle, the empathy between fellow beekeepers, and the therapeutic peace he derives from tending his colonies in the glorious Cotswold countryside.

The Custodians
and the Manor House

Over the last 30 years a couple have conserved and repaired their Tudor manor house. They share it with their five children and, during the summer months, with weekly visitors who tour the house.

left The oak parlour (dated 1616) is the original lord's parlour situated at the upper end of the Tudor hall. The camel-backed sofa is piled high with Turkish and Greek kilim cushions.

right A wooden staircase, with some original timber baulk steps, leads to a garret haunted by four benign ghosts. The seventeenth-century monk's shoe was found under floorboards near the drawing-room fireplace in 1925.

It is rare to find a house and garden today that, without being showpieces, are so steeped in distant history. In 1924 a young American architect, Francis Comstock, made meticulous measured drawings of the house and described it as "by far the most perfect manor house in all of England". Before the 1920s the house and estate had been in the same family for nearly a thousand years. However, it was uninhabited for over one hundred of those years (1815–1925), when a new, and grander, family mansion was built on a nearby hill and it became used instead for picnics and after-church excursions for the family's weekend house parties.

When Cotswold Arts-and-Crafts man Norman Jewson bought the estate with nine acres for £3,200 in 1925 he resolved to repair and restore it to its former glory. The Cotswold Arts

left A French chair, dating from 1680, sits alongside a family dressing case on which lies a Tibetan hat collected during the family's travels abroad.

below left A plum-coloured, cut-velvet coat, minus collar and buttons, with long vents and deep, lace-fringed cuffs is displayed beside an 1895 oak table by Sidney Barnsley, a member of the Arts and Crafts movement.

right Although considered by experts as the valueless detritus of the Victorian period, the custodians regard these bottles and pots as precious remnants from the estate's past.

and Crafts movement, which had been underway since the end of the nineteenth century at Kelmscott Manor under William Morris, believed in conservative repair and the use of local materials. At the manor house a team of local craftsmen were employed, and damaged floorboards in the oak parlour were replaced by elm sawn from a local mill. Jewson created a number of watercolour sketches and detailed drawings, some of which still hang in the house.

The existing Cotswold-stone manor house has grown organically through additions from east to west over a period of three centuries. The oldest part is the east wing. Its arch-

left At the top of the first flight of stairs a small bathroom, previously a dressing room, faces towards the Church of the Holy Cross, which stands just above the manor house.

right The Little Parlour, painted by Francis Moss Bennett in 1922. To the left of the door, which leads into the central Tudor hall, is an eighteenth-century walnut secretaire and a William and Mary armchair.

overleaf The main south façade of the manor faces the valley – the three irregular gables are nearly a century apart in date. The church, behind, has medieval origins but a Victorian decorative interior of tiles and mosaics, considered the richest of its kind in the Cotswolds.

braced, cruck trusses to the south end of the roof date it as fifteenth century, as do the windows, which were "pierced" into the facade. The central section, containing the hall, is mid-sixteenth-century, made from local rubble stone and rendered with lime and horsehair. The window dressings, quoins, lintels, coping stones, and finials are constructed from Cotswold freestone. Above the hall is "Queen Margaret's room", so-called because Queen Margaret of Anjou, wife of Henry VI, stayed here in 1471.

The west section dates from 1616 and contains the oak parlour. The wood panelling here is one of the earliest surviving examples; Norman Jewson's Arts and Crafts elm floor is tapered, the boards laid alternately – dovetail fashion. Above the parlour is the Solar room. This bedroom is the principal first-floor chamber of the early seventeenth-century manor, with views across the formal parterre garden with its early Georgian gate piers and yew parlour.

Beadwork collected by a family ancestor sits in a cabinet by Harry Davoll at the foot of the bed, and hanging from a wardrobe is a child's late-Victorian/Edwardian fancy-dress costume. The house is unique for retaining the Tudor and Stuart answer to wallpaper – cloths painted in distemper. A cheaper substitute for tapesteries, the technique was similar to that employed for stage scenery or festival banners. They illustrate scenes from the Bible of the life of Joseph and his brothers.

Had it not been for the work of Norman Jewson the manor house may well have fallen into irrevocable disrepair. The custodians continue his example but use the house as a fully functioning family home too. Visitors can see "workmanship of different dates co-existing harmoniously, and seventeenth- and eighteenth-century furnishings blending easily with later things in the manner prized by the Arts and Crafts movement". The custodians ensure that it is one of the few houses left in England where genuine old-English style can be appreciated and shared by visitors in its original context.

The Sculptress
and the Hunting Lodge

The Domesday Book of 1086 recorded the Cotswold's Wychwood Forest as a Royal forest. For the last eleven years a family has lived in a beautiful seventeeth-century house built on the site of one of the original Royal hunting lodges.

Despite a green oak extension to the kitchen, which has created a large family room, and an exchange of front and back doors, the hunting lodge still bears many of the characteristics of its seventeenth-century past, when hunting parties were regularly held here.

The current hallway was once a game larder – sturdy hooks for hanging game still run the length of an ancient beam. Hefty locks and bolts, an intrinsic part of the original wooden doors, were necessary then to prevent poachers stealing the hunters' spoils. In the original front porch, where the front door used to be, iron rings are fixed into the wall where gun dogs were tied up during shooting lunches. In the kitchen a large bread oven produced sufficient numbers of loaves to feed the villagers; locals trod a well-worn path across the fields to collect their "daily bread" from a sliding window at the back of the lodge.

left The south-west facing façade used to be the front entrance. The Stonesfield slate roof tiles are graded traditionally by size and named after birds. Old-fashioned roses, lavender, rosemary, and wisteria blur the straight edges of the Cotswold stone.

right Entitled *Time Out*, this reclining figure is an example of one of the sculptress' earlier pieces, made from fired clay. It occupies windowsill space in the studio.

below right Beneath a mahogany Victorian bench, on an original stone-flagged floor, is a collection of tucked away, "less than favourite" pieces reflecting experiments with patination (colour). The wallpaper is trompe l'oeil wood panelling.

The present incumbents were initially drawn to this part of rural England some 20 years ago. Their chosen area of the Cotswolds was close to civilization but still wide of the beaten track. The lush, undulating countryside, haphazardly divided by dry-stone walls and punctuated by the uniform tones of church towers, steep gables, and stone-slated roofs, also appealed. By coming to the Cotswolds the sculptress and her husband fulfilled a dream of bringing up their children among fields and streams, granting them the space to breathe.

Ten years spent at home in the company of her young, growing family inspired the subject matter for much of the sculptress' pieces – especially early examples. On two walls in the kitchen are circular terracotta plaques entitled *Trinity*, which depict a mother, father, and baby; on the floor in the family room is a clay model of a mother, her arms encircling a small child, called *All-Embracing Love*. Where other families pepper their houses with photographic evidence of their children's childhood years, the sculptress' downstairs rooms are alive with three-dimensional records of her sons and daughters, forever captured reclining on windowsills or reading books on mantelpieces. More recently, larger lifesize pieces requiring armatures and cast in bronze resin have joined the collection. One entitled *Layed Back*, lying full stretch on a dry-stone wall in the garden, will be lastingly reminiscent of her son aged ten years.

A studio, bathed in natural overhead light, recently has been created within the house so that materials and tools are on hand, enabling the sculptress to be inspired spontaneously by her idyllic home surroundings.

left In front of the fireplace in the green oak extension family room is one of the artist's favourite pieces, *Joie de Vivre*. Comfortable sofas and chairs furnish the room but cushions are in short supply as the family's dog often removes them.

right This elegant piece, *Woman Stretching*, has been made from bronze resin and is smooth and sensuous, inviting touch. The artist likes to suggest anatomical correctness but is more interested in "evoking feeling and mood".

below right The sculptress' recently constructed studio, which doubles up as the laundry room, is lit naturally from the gallery above. On the workbench are her tools and any work in progress.

The Garden Designer
and the Manor

The Garden Designer grew up in the heart of the
Oxfordshire Cotswolds and confesses an irresistible
affinity with the area. He and his family live in a
steeply gabled manor around which he has created
a beautiful two-acre garden.

When the garden designer and his wife bought the manor back in 1992 the bones of a garden were already there. The garden had existing compartments that worked, and their predecessors had chosen good shrubs, old-fashioned roses, and beech hedges and trees. However, the garden designer and his wife are responsible for all the hard landscaping such as paths and steps, as well as renewing and re-planting areas of the garden. One gravel path leads between low box hedging and beneath iron arches, thickly entangled by the roses *Phyllis Bide* and *Alister Stella Gray*, to the greenhouse and to a fortress created for the children with a box hedge that has been castellated to blend in. Portuguese laurels (*prunus lusitanica*) were also inherited from the previous owners but the garden designer cut them back hard several years ago. The regrowth has been clipped tightly into an evergreen pyramid now worthy of the title "moorish tower".

above The west-facing kitchen looks out onto terracotta pots containing white petunias. The walls are adorned with a selection of family photographs.

right A view through an arch from the entrance hall into the drawing room, where seventeenth-century oak beams support the ceiling and the floor is stone flagged.

The stone house sits east and well forward of its plot, and is almost totally concealed beneath magnolia, climbing roses, clematis, and lilac. Throughout the year the garden designer's wife, who has a dislike for bought, cut flowers, is able to fill the house with natural arrangements supplied by plants growing in various parts of the garden. Both husband and wife agree that a "cutting garden" is not necessary for a modest family house. Plants in pots are also a passion for the garden designer's wife, herself an experienced and knowledgable gardener. They adorn terraces beyond the kitchen window and, arranged on brick supports, create shapes and colours of various heights around the front and back doors, whatever the time of year. Terracotta pots are collected from a local Cotswold company.

left In the drawing room a damask, camel-backed sofa has cushions embroidered with auriculas, lilies, and daises by the garden designer's sister-in-law and godmother. Outside, *rosa raubritter*, clematis *texensis*, and white lilac frame the window.

below Upstairs, in a daughter's bedroom, an Indian rocking horse looks out from between the nineteenth-century oak cupboard and a bedroom chair with teddies and cushions covered in French *Toile de Jouy* material.

Within the house is evidence of the presence of four growing children: a wooden banquette around the kitchen table contains football boots, and beside the back door are gumboots of various sizes, baskets bulging with cricket balls and footballs, and childrens' tools and trowels protruding from aluminium pails. Now that the children are older, they are able to help with some supervised mowing and strimming.

The preference for traditional, formally structured gardens that also express individual flair extends into the house. Original features – such as seventeenth-century beams, stone-mullioned windows, and flagstoned floors – frame rooms containing family furniture alongside eclectic pieces gathered from around the world. Against the varnished coral-pink walls of the hall a striking "Harlequin" bust, bought from the summer exhibition at the Royal Academy of Arts in London, resides among more traditional pieces and pictures. In the drawing room fringed Spanish material frames a window overlooking the garden, and substantial blue-and-white Chinese ginger jars sit on a windowsill behind an elegant damask camel-backed sofa. Fresh flowers from the garden, a prevalent feature in the house, fill an English slop pail, and embroidered cushions depicting auriculas, lilies, and daisies ensure that, even inside, "outside" is uppermost.

left Wooden wine boxes are used to hold rolls of garden plans created on tracing paper. The garden designer creates watercolours for all his garden drawings.

below left The garden designer's office sits above the kitchen, with views of the garden to the west. A stained-pine circular desk is supported on four filing cabinets.

right In the hall a grandfather clock and large-scale seascape of Aldeburgh, Suffolk, adorn gesso-red varnished walls. Beside a Royal College of Needlework chair depicting the family coat of arms reclines the family's chocolate labrador.

The garden designer's study, previously a playroom, is situated on the first floor and overlooks the west side of the garden. The room is painted green and pictures are consciously restricted to black-and-white prints only. Once established within the circumference of his circular desk the garden designer is able to plan and write his lectures and be in close contact with his clients. The tools of his trade – reference books, drawing equipment stored in old cigar boxes, and a drawing board lit by a high-tech remote control light – are also all within easy reach. Detailed plans for clients appear on tracing paper, and impressions of how their gardens will look are painted meticulously in watercolours. As with the finished products, these plans themselves are works of art.

Although an informed theorist, the garden designer recognized the importance of hands-on experience. He spent twelve months as head gardener of a much-photographed

left Opposite the manor's back door an Indian sandstone path leads to a teak garden bench against a barn tiled with Cotswold Stonesfield slate. The barn wall is covered by vines, clematis *tangutica*, and the pink rose *Baroness Rothschild*.

right A love of pesto sauce, requiring quantities of fresh basil, pine nuts, parmesan cheese, and olive oil, has inititated the growing of Genoese sweet basil from seed in wooden wine cases.

four-acre garden on top of the Berkshire Downs, and followed that with a significant stint selling rare and unusual perennials and bulbs from a nursery in Longworth, Oxfordshire. He has gone on to lecture on the history of gardens from the seventeenth to the twentieth century for the National Association of Decorative and Fine Art Societies (NADFAS) and for Middlesex University, as well as developing a long client list of those keen for him to design their own private gardens.

The garden designer has specific preferences and branches of expertise. He is obsessed with vistas and views and, possibly on account of his lecturing background, prefers working with older period houses and creating traditional gardens that are structured and slightly formal. He is also budget-sensitive, and both perceptive and receptive to his clients' wishes. Within his own garden he is constantly experimenting with plant forms and shapes that are not only beautiful but also necessarily resilient to dogs, chickens, and footballs. Practical considerations are often at the forefront of gardens designed for clients, and "low maintenance" features high up on the criteria list.

Nevertheless, his designs have flair and imagination and new ideas are constantly evolving; his current passion is to have gold somewhere in the garden to create unexpected flashes of light. Within his own garden he is creating plant supports from two metal wigwams, which he intends to gild and surmount with steel balls. In the vegetable garden birch tree-trunks are washed in autumn to ensure decorative "white" trunks during the winter.

The Bookbinder
and the Chapel House

In an old Methodist chapel house in the southern sphere of the Cotswolds, the architectural style is less typical. It is home to an artistic and creative family of five: the father makes furniture, while the mother practises the skilled and unusual art of bookbinding.

The southern half of the Cotswolds contains the hamlet of Kelmscott, birthplace of the Arts and Crafts movement, so it is appropriate that a bookbinder and her husband, himself a prolific and imaginative wood-worker, should have made their home in the area. The Old Chapel House is so-called because a Wesleyian Methodist chapel used to stand in its garden and the house served as home to a succession of ministers and their families.

It is not a typical Cotswold-stone house. Made of fox-red brick and of symmetrical Georgian proportions, it is a handsome village house whose front door opens directly onto the village thoroughfare. Large windows allow light to flood into each well-proportioned room. The enclosed back garden, laid to lawn, is large enough for three boys and their father to practise football. A steady stream of neighbouring children habitually infiltrate the house.

The bookbinder remembers that a rural house in the middle of fields was what they originally had in mind 15 years ago when they went househunting with a small baby. Not only was the chapel house in the wrong location, it was a "bombsite" – daylight could be seen through its walls. But the appeal lay in the balanced proportions of the main rooms and the economical use of space, there being no narrow corridors. The hall and steep,

right In the main bedroom, the bookbinder's husband has made a tall oak cupboard to fit a niche in the wall. A French bench, bought locally, shares room space with a tall-backed, irregularly shaped chair home-crafted from driftwood.

below left The main staircase leads directly onto a landing bathroom on the top floor, where the beams of the house, angled door frame, and sloping ceilings create striking diamond shapes.

left The kitchen is reflective of the clean, linear style perpetrated by the bookbinder's husband – the table, chairs, kitchen cupboards, and shelves have all been made by him.

right In the bookbinder's workroom a large portrait by the artist Silas Birtwistle, framed in oak by the bookbinder's husband, dominates the wall space. Paper, hand-sewn to tape, is waiting to be bound on the workbench .

white wooden staircase that leads from it to two upstairs storeys are central, in the style of a Georgian doll's house. The scuffed paint on the stairs pays testimony to the heavy flow of traffic, and throughout the house there's evidence of artistic creativity.

The bookbinder's husband is a wood-worker. He fights shy of the "furniture designer" tag, arguing that he doesn't always draw his designs first but makes them spontaneously once he's established the basic measurements. Describing his work as "simple and linear", there is evidence of it throughout the kitchen, within the structure of the new conservatory, in picture frames, and in the Arts-and-Crafts-style bed in the master bedroom.

Further along the wood-processing chain, the bookbinder restores and creates beautiful books in a light, high-ceilinged room adjacent to the conservatory and kitchen. An evening class in bookbinding led to a job restoring old books that has now evolved into a flourishing home-based business restoring books and creating from scratch new albums, notebooks,

left Within a thick wooden lay press an old book is awaiting restoration; others of assorted shapes and sizes are piled in the background. Heat tools for transferring images and lettering onto spines lie across the press.

below left New books can be used as photo albums, notebooks, or visitor's books. The bookbinder departs from traditional marbled covers – her colour combinations and embossed designs are strikingly bold.

right In the drawing room warm colours are introduced with rugs, Indian cushions, and tartan arm rests. Above the wood-burning stove a collection of Eric Ravilious china mugs decorates the mantelpiece, surmounted by an Adam Birtwistle painting.

and visitor's books, beautifully bound in colourful cloth embossed with gold-leaf designs. The bookbinder's love of colour occasionally is reflected inside the house, in a bright kilim rug, bedcover, or pair of curtains, but, overall, neutral tones win the day.

Within the workroom is an orderly sense of traditional industry. A wooden filing chest of small drawers sits on a bench made by her husband. It contains the many strangely named tools of her trade – "spoke shaves", "bone-folders", water stones, paring and heat tools, gold leaf, and alphabets. Collapsed spines on old books are skilfully replaced with new curved ones to avoid a book's precious contents pressing directly onto surfaces; old Bibles frequently reside in wooden presses awaiting treatment. In the chapel house clutter is not permitted. The white painted stairs, central to the house's structure, are also reflective of a core style of clean simplicity that pervades throughout.

The Teacher
and the Farmhouse

At her eighteenth-century Georgian farmhouse the teacher shows groups of children how to develop and enjoy their artistic skills amid all the traditionally English rural props – animals, trees, fields, and farmyards.

left The teacher's husband designed the simple stone fireplace in the hall, on which stands a collection of contemporary earthenware pottery.

right In the drawing room ripe corn-coloured walls are offset by ivory linen curtains that were originally heavy-duty linen bedsheets from France. French ticking material is used to make cushions and window seats.

During half-term holidays, and throughout the long summer break, parents follow directions from the Cotswold town of Burford, through fields and hamlets of wisteria-clad, ochre-coloured stone buildings, to a rendezvous at a beautifully renovated farmhouse behind a Norman church. A garden of mown grass, a rose walk, football nets, and a tree whose branches grow horizontally and close to the ground (making it an ideal "camp") border the house on one side; on the other side of the house, through an arch, is a small stable block and beyond it a sweeping valley of pasture land criss-crossed by Cotswold stone walls. Parents leave their children here with picnic lunches, sometimes for the whole day, where they will be in the capable and creative hands of the teacher who lives here. Themed workshop days vary in title from "Knight School", "Wild West", "Treasure Chest", and "Fish and Ships", to days designed for a child's birthday around his or her specific interests.

The teacher has had extensive practical training. An amalgamation of two marriages resulted in eight children beneath the age of fourteen. The house was bought 13 years ago to accommodate them all, and a process of gradual renovation has resulted in a home that is practical and flexible. The oldest part, dating from the mid-eighteenth century, is a dining

right A French bedframe, found in a local antique shop, has been re-painted in Farrow and Ball's "Old White" and covered in antique white-linen bedding. Material collected from a château in France was made into 480 squares and sewn together by the teacher to make the beautiful patchwork curtains.

left Through an arch on the north side of the house, pupils explore a stable block and visit Cobweb, the small 36-year old pony on which all the family learnt to ride.

below left Cobweb comes into the house at Christmas and attends many workshop days. He is led into the studio via the garden door and becomes the focus for a day with an equine theme, or acts as a pack-horse carrying packed lunches to woodland forts or shipwreck camps.

right The south-facing façade of the Georgian farmhouse looks onto a garden of mown grass, herbaceous borders, and a pleached hornbeam walk. The stone-tiled roof has been pierced by dormer windows opening into an attic room, which runs the length of the house.

room that doubles up to become the teacher's studio. The table's height adjusts upwards and downwards depending on the age and size of the children in the class.

The teacher and her family holiday in a house in rural south-west France, and evidence of that country's textiles and artifacts are prevalent throughout the house. A favourite pastime is to go to the French equivalent of car-boot sales (*vide greniers*, which loosely translates as "empty attics"). Upstairs in the main bedroom fragments of French material have been

sewn together to form patchwork curtains, and the magnificent double bed's frame, painted a soft putty-grey, is surmounted by crisp, white antique French bedding. An Edwardian fireplace is adorned with coffee cups found in French *brocante* markets and a French sewing kit. Beside the fireplace an old box bearing the word *Cusenier* is used for logs.

The house throughout is reflective of a background steeped in design and order that is attributable both to the teacher and to her husband who, as an architect, has a flair for using space to maximum advantage. The lines are clean and uncluttered, and rural tones (ochre yellows, soft greys, warm terracottas, and corals) synchronized with neutral ivory linens and natural textures (wicker, stone, timber, and terracotta tiles) prevail in the hall and drawing room. However, in the studio/dining room, the palate becomes sharper. Simple white shelves either side of the fireplace are filled with chipped, incomplete sets of Art Deco Clarice Cliff china, loved for its citrus colours.

An artistic background and a vivid imagination constantly fuels the teacher's ideas for new workshops. A flair for lettering and layout means that those ideas are successfully and practically expressed, and objects made by the children to take home are well-presented and properly made. But the long-term legacy of the teacher's themed workshops in her Cotswold home lies in the stimulation of young minds amid the peace and tranquillity of rural life, and in the confidence acquired from creating something worthwhile and durable.

The Farmer
and the Cottages

Two early-Victorian agricultural cottages knocked together into one is home to the sheep farmer and his family. For twenty-five years he has continued the age-old agricultural tradition that has been followed in the Cotswolds since pre-Roman times.

When the sheep farmer inherited his father's 170 acres of farm he was 24 years old and newly married; he now farms 500 acres. His wife was born in Jersey but she has grown to love her marital home in the Cotswolds, with its huge skyscapes, views of rolling pasture and stone walls, and the wild expanses of Cleeve Hill, juxtaposed with the cultural attractions of nearby Cheltenham.

When they inherited the "house" it was still two separate cottages. Over the years, as the family has grown, they have spread into both buildings, knocking through and renovating them. The work was done on a shoestring, shared between the sheep farmer (he made all the doors in the house from reclaimed pine) and his brother, a builder. Felled chestnut from around the farm was used to create kitchen worktops, and an oak tree forms a beam above the Aga. When a windfall allowed them to extend the house they voted against a south-facing garden terrace in preference of installing the Aga cooker in the kitchen –

above The kitchen table doubles up as the farmer's office. Modern farmers are overrun by paperwork; he is also chairman of the Cotswold Sheep Group.

right The kitchen is a central focus for cooking large meals for the family and for students working during the busy spring lambing period.

previous page At the south-west end of the house is the farmer's drawing room where a fire is lit most nights using fallen timber from the farm. A glass-fronted cabinet displays fossils collected locally.

left The opposite end of the kitchen looks out on the steeply sloping garden containing the vegetable patch. A comfortable chair, cushioned with an old Welsh blanket, is ideal for late-night reading.

right A teenage daughter's bedroom is refreshingly traditional: her grandfather's hunting horn sits on the windowsill and an inherited paisley eiderdown covers the bed.

a valuable element in their rural lifestyle. Hypothermic lambs are warmed up in the cooler bottom oven, and large family meals are offered to the student workers who help during the busy lambing season in spring.

The annual sheep-farming cycle begins in autumn, when work focuses on ensuring that all 1,300 ewes are in supreme condition before meeting the rams in November. During the later winter months the ewes are sheared before being herded into sheltered barns. Not only does this provide the ewes with a warm, protected environment but it also ensures that the fields are rested and that fresh, green pasture will grow in the spring.

The first batch of lambing occurs in January, and again in March and April. The farmer's wife shares the early-morning shifts, checking for newborns and feeding orphaned lambs. Early summer is dominated by harvesting the grass crops to create hay and silage. Throughout the year sheep must be sheared and fences, gates, and stone walls maintained. The farmer is aided in his work by his three sheep dogs. Reared as puppies, their training begins at eighteen months when they are taught the necessary skills of rounding up, separating, and "funnelling" the sheep.

The kitchen is certainly the heart of this house. The farmer, who is also chairman of the Cotswold Sheep Group, works through the ubiquitous paperwork on the kitchen table; a floral armchair, in one corner, is a good spot for late-night reading. A collection of bright-blue chemists' bottles adorn the windowsill beside the chair and above, on the walls, are framed

left The south end of
the house is bordered by
Cotswold-stone walls. It
overlooks nothing but grass-
land and the neighbouring
farm across "Fat Valley".

below left After a day's
game-shooting the sheep
farmer cleans his gun in the
boot room and replaces it in
its original red, felt-lined case.

right The boot room leads
into the house via a stable
door. Muddy boots, a lamb-
skin waistcoat, and a sheep
crook are frequently discarded
here. Lanterns and torches
are vital for checking the
sheep are safe at night.

photographs of plants and leaves by the celebrated photographer Fay Godwin. Near the Aga
is a colourful Mexican embroidery and beneath it, on the worktop, a "back" sculpture by the
farmer's teenage daughter. The style of the room is reflective of a family's travels and
experiences. There are no curtains at the windows but the view across the valley from the
kitchen's front window is spectacular. Inside there is a constant sense of "outside".

Previously at the back of the house, the kitchen now extends the depth of the building
so that its front window has a clear outlook over "Fat Valley", so called by the Romans
because of the fertility of its soil – the Romans grew vineyards and tobacco there. A metal
detector led to the discovery of a Bronze Age coin, a coin from Charles 1's reign, and a
Victorian coin all on the same morning. It seems testimony to the continuing life of man
against an ancient rural back-drop.

The Knitwear Designer
and the Miller's House

On the site of an eleventh-century mill, a house
on three floors was built in the nineteenth century
for a miller and his servants. Facing south towards
Kingham across the Evenlode valley, it is now the
home of a knitwear designer and her family.

The knitwear designer's Cotswold way of life is many miles from her Australian birthplace, but her passion for knitting, learnt as a small child from her grandmother, has stayed with her. The creative work ethic was an integral part of the knitwear designer's upbringing: her mother made the family's school jumpers on knitting machines shared by neighbours, her cousins embroidered, and, as a family, they spun together on a portable spinner. The garments she now produces – hats, scarves, coats, waistcoats, and cardigans – are characteristically vibrant and intricately patterned using wool and cotton chenille, which gives them a distinctive, embossed texture.

The creation of new designs follows a specific cycle, beginning in autumn when the knitwear designer spends two weeks drawing in her home studio, followed by pattern-making. For inspiration she visits the Victoria and Albert Museum's library and the National

left Handpainted plates and vases, often a source of knitwear inspiration for their rich colours and intricate patterns, sit on the teak sideboard in the kitchen.

above Wall-to-ceiling pigeon holes in the designer's offices accommodate rolls of brightly coloured yarn. Mending, pressing, and labelling take place here prior to despatch.

Portrait Gallery in London, to absorb the richly decorated medieval fabrics seen in Venetian and Florentine Renaissance paintings. Throughout the house are well-thumbed piles of hardbacked picture books featuring coloured prints of artists' work; Matisse's clarity of colour and the business of his patterns are a frequent influence. Other sources of inspiration include Indian embroideries, kilim rugs, and Elizabethan crewel work. All are prevalent throughout the house, as are original handpainted ceramics by artists who trained at the Royal College of Art, such as the English Delft china arranged above the original brick fireplace in the kitchen.

From offices situated, appropriately, within a medieval wool-merchant's hall in nearby Burford, the knitwear designer's husband ensures that her designs are commercially produced and sold, not just locally and in the UK, but all over the world. She has a workshop within the offices, piled high with coloured yarns. At her knitting machine she experiments with intricate combinations until satisfied that nothing jars the eye. It is a process that can't be done on paper, only with the wool itself, in the same fashion as her medieval Cotswold predecessors.

above A view from the breakfast room to the south-facing garden room. Kenyan baskets, kilim bags, and handpainted china inform and inspire many of the knitwear designs.

right During a recent renovation of the kitchen old bread ovens were discovered, as well as an indentation from the feet of people who stood habitually in the same place to knead the dough.

left A yellow north-facing bedroom overlooks the garden. The double quilt, made from assorted blue fabrics collected from the USA, was created by the knitwear designer, as were the framed cross-stitch wall samplers.

below left A working table in the studio has been handpainted acid yellow. Books lining the shelves above the desk focus on the art of old Venetian and Florentine masters and the work of the artist Matisse.

right Piled beneath the window between the garden room and the drawing room are beautiful patchwork quilts made by the knitwear designer. Their creation and production emerged from an initial desire to keep her children warm as babies during the long winter months.

The Carpenter

and the Cow Byre

In a late-eighteenth century agricultural barn,
originally used for threshing corn and wintering
cattle, a carpenter has created, almost single-
handedly, a unique house for his family. It took
ten years to build but the results are spectacular.

Encircled by Norway spruces against a steep hillside, a stone cow byre looks as if it has evolved geologically from its landscape. In its lush valley of pasture and woodland, the main view, facing east, contains nothing man-made as far as the eye can see. The oldest alder tree in England (750 years old) stands in its immediate sphere. In this north-west corner of the southern Cotswolds, captured by Laurie Lee in his autobiographical book *Cider with Rosie*, the rural outlook appears to be caught in a timewarp.

The cow byre and adjoining barn, on land previously owned and farmed by the carpenter's family, were bought dilapidated and full of nettles in 1988, soon after the carpenter and his wife were married. His mother labelled them "hopeless romantics". Acquiring planning permission was long and tedious and only awarded eventually on appeal. But as the son of an inventor of agricultural machinery, and the grandson of the first woman to receive an agricultural degree from Cambridge, it seems unlikely that the carpenter would have been thwarted by bureaucracy.

Gradually, with building underway, the carpenter's farming career surrendered to the full-time project of construction and renovation. In return for somewhere to pitch their wagons, travellers – themselves skilled craftsmen – helped with aspects of the building, particularly

right The internal design of the house and its floor levels were determined by how the house would appear within the landscape. Looking through an arched door from the sitting room, the central hall doubles as a music room.

below left The front door leads into a hall laid with Cotswold-stone slabs salvaged from Sheepscombe church. All the doors are designed around ironwork collected by the carpenter, including old latches, locks, and nails.

the roof, which took a year and a half. Beams were sought not from timber merchants but from fallen oak and ash trees in local woodlands; stone tiles, removed and stacked in the barn during World War II, were carefully re-laid. Through a charitable local network 55 square yards of stone slabs, ideal for floors, were located and salvaged from Sheepscombe church. Basins were found in an old nunnery, and a stone trough was used in the downstairs shower. A beautiful 400-year-old Cotswold door frame was lowered to form a fireplace in the drawing room, where it provides a central focus.

If he couldn't find what he needed the carpenter disassembled elements found in listed buildings and copied them. Stairs were made from solid blocks of oak, and stair rails "turned" to emulate the diamond angles of carthorse hay mangers. Doors were pointed in lime mortar, as seen in Gloucester cathedral.

left The master bathroom has far-reaching views across the valley of rolling pasture and tree-capped hills, through windows designed and installed by the carpenter.

above Looking south to the north facades of the converted cow byre and threshing barn illustrates how unobtrusively they sit in their landscape, surrounded by spruce trees.

right In the drawing room a beautiful and ancient Cotswold-stone door-frame, discovered locally, has been lowered to form a stunning fire surround. The solid block of wood above the curve-topped doorway acquired its "aged" appearance by being burnt and wire brushed.

From an early age the carpenter has collected old hinges and bolts, some over 400 years old, from reclamation yards or car boot (garage) sales. In his workshop he has accumulated a hoard sufficient for three houses. Treasured gems are latches and other ironwork made by a Cotswold craftsman, Norman Bucknell, whose designs are characteristically "finished" and "filed". All the doors in the cow byre have been made by the carpenter, save one – an old Gothic door made during the Arts and Crafts movement at the end of the nineteenth century.

For ten years the house has been evolving as though it were a fully dimensional sculpture; internal designs have been planned and dictated by how the house would look on the outside, from all vistas. Finally now the carpenter has the time to take new furniture commissions.

right The sitting room leads out onto a south-facing stone-cobbled log store, which also serves as a sheltered winter and summer sitting area. Boots, sticks, and hats reflect the family's habitual love of walking in the surrounding Cotswold countryside.

below left Felled oak and ash, rescued from nearby woodland, was used to create the beams and kitchen cupboards; the table was made by the carpenter from a large oak tree. The turquoise cupboard was shipped from Bali.

The Writer

and the Folly

A writer and her family live in a farmhouse built in
the late-eighteenth century as an "eye-catcher", or
"folly", for the titled family of the "big house" to see
across the open parkland of their rural retreat. The
environment provides rich inspiration for writing.

Ten years ago a writer stumbled across a folly while out walking with a friend. Standing in the middle of open countryside, with 360 degree views and not another house in sight, its location and unusual architecture stirred a romantic chord that refused to be silenced. From a practical point of view the project seemed insurmountable. The house is two-faced: one side presents as a partially restored medieval castle, complete with sham twin towers, arrow slits, and ecclesiastical lights; the other as a lean-to farmhouse, with spiral staircases and long, thin corridors. The house is only one-room deep, with a series of warren-like rooms leading one from another like the carriages on a train. The cobbled yard on the farmhouse side was covered in concrete and discarded corrugated iron.

However, the writer and her husband had spent time in France and Italy and were drawn to external building features that were reminiscent of Provence. While friends eulogized about the "castle" façade, the couple were visualizing the dilapidated farmyard as a glorious

above A door leads directly from the red library onto rising layers of open countryside and parkland. Castellations on the edges of the bookshelves echo the house's architecture.

right Six doors lead out of the small library, one into a mint-green and denim-blue dining room, where shelves carry the family's collection of inherited china and glass.

south-facing garden shared by children and animals. Inside they were enchanted by French shutters, wooden panelling, and floors of timber, stone, and terracotta. The windows varied from leaded, to sash, to casement. Walls were thick and windowsills deeply recessed.

When they acquired the house in 1996 they spent six months making it habitable; four bathrooms and a kitchen had to be installed. Belfast sinks, freestanding cast-iron baths, and loos with capacious wooden seats were chosen over modern alternatives. A conscious decision was made to use paint colours and furniture reflecting robust and rural practicality in the servicable end of the house, encompassing the kitchen, breakfast room, utility, and boot rooms. Colours in the kitchen are reminiscent of milk and clotted cream, and work units are simple and unfussy. The kitchen leads directly onto the cobbled south-facing courtyard. A solid external door has been replaced by a half-glazed stable door so that light floods into the kitchen and there are clear, uninterrupted views of the distant White Horse Hill.

At the other end of the house, now containing a library, a dining room, a drawing room, and a lean-to conservatory, the writer and her husband endeavoured to evoke the rich medieval qualities of the castle façade by choosing vibrant colour schemes. Decorative details were introduced with cushions of different textures and patterns, china and glass, and large-scale

left A large bathroom with a south-facing sash window has an old-fashioned, free-standing cast iron bath. Blue-and-white striped curtains, made from material found in a French Provencal market, echo the cornflower-blue half-panelling on the walls.

below left A daughter's bedroom has views across open parkland through a pair of windows that appear as medieval arrow slits on the north-facing façade. The colours are bold and bright.

right Surplus strips of wooden castellation from the library have been added to an existing bedroom wardrobe. Bare pale-blue floorboards, white walls, and fresh blue-and-white colour schemes, juxtaposed with robust oak furniture, create a sense of rural Italy.

gilt-framed pictures and mirrors. Bookshelves were created topped by castellations to echo the castle theme. Throughout, simple linen curtains were made to hang from cast-iron poles, reminiscent of rural Umbria. The writer's husband is passionate about the different blues used in France for shutters. He chose the bold cornflower-blue paint for the wooden half-panelling in one bathroom. On the third floor, accessed by two separate spiral staircases, the three children's rooms display a similar penchant for bright colour.

For the writer the charm of the house lies in its peacefulness and the inspiration provided by the rural landscape. Writer's block is temporarily overcome by walking into the surrounding countryside. There are no restrictions: favoured routes wind through woods, along headlands, across stubble fields, or via farm tracks and footpaths. Her next project is fiction – four chapters are already underway. The writer is able to work late into the night, her preferred time of working, so long as she is respectful. The house, beyond a certain time of night, is almost certainly haunted.

below Gilt-framed family portraits and furniture in warm reds and golds compliment the wheat-coloured French wallpaper embossed with gold and red circles.

right A view of the castellated roof, spiral staircases with arrow slits, and bow-fronted additions. Geese, dogs, hens, and a cat live in cosy harmony in the cobbled courtyard.

The Antiques Collector
and the Farmhouse

A yeoman's farmhouse, with flagstoned floors, stone-mullioned windows, low upstairs ceilings, and a steeply gabled attic that runs the length of the house, has been in the same family for three generations. The current incumbent is an antiques dealer.

Such was the reputation of the Cotswold Arts and Crafts movement at the beginning of the twentieth century, that a Winchester College housemaster, whose hobby was amateur woodworking, was drawn to the Thames Valley. He bought a rural farmhouse within the heart of the movement's sphere. Over the centuries the house, the core of which is seventeenth-century with a Georgian south-west wing, had evolved in a traditional way. Evidence of the schoolmaster's woodwork (principally in oak, and based on traditional, vernacular designs) is everywhere. Beneath a gilt-framed portrait of him in the entrance hall is a large carved-oak settle; in the Oak Room a bookcase reminiscent of Renaissance designs lines one wall; he also instigated the oak panelling in the dining room.

All the outbuildings have evolved across the centuries in the same way as the house. A stable contains original stalls, and a grainstore above the old cart shed has been a furniture workshop for the schoolmaster, his nephew (another carpenter), and now the nephew's son, the antiques collector, who uses the space for waxing, polishing, and "finishing" items of furniture before their sale. Inside, a heady mix of spirits, polish, and sawn timber assails visitors' nostrils; the combination is reminiscent of ecclesiastical interiors. From the ordered collections of tools and materials there is a strong sense of past and present. Saws

right At the library end of the Oak Room are wall-length bookshelves made by the antique dealer's great-uncle. Beside a Regency drum table is a Regency *bergere* library chair.

below A stone-mullioned window above the kitchen sink originates from the earliest, seventeenth-century part of the house. It is flanked by trompe l'oeil shutters.

left On a windowsill is a collection of German stoneware "Bellarmine" jugs, so called because grotesque masks of the brutal Italian cardinal, Bellarmino, adorn their necks.

below left A latched door to the right of the Aga opens onto an original elm staircase. The antique dealer's father made the kitchen table from Italian walnut during a period of convalescence in Italy during World War II.

right The carved oak settle in the front hall is a typical example of the great-uncle's oak woodwork; above it hangs his portrait.

previous page At the fireplace-end of the Oak Room a Knole sofa, covered in terracotta-coloured velvet, fills the space beneath the window. A large "Turkey" rug covers the floor and the painted, bow-fronted corner cupboard is eighteenth-century Italian.

left Above the bath-surround of black marble is a collection of six Japanese prints. An Irish-glass beaded mirror surmounts the basin, and to one side is a Victorian, metal-based mahogany table.

right In a bedroom with an original Cotswold moulded-stone fireplace is the walnut knee-hole desk made by the antique dealer's father. A leather stationery box sits on the desk.

of every size hang from beams; moulding planes (one bearing the schoolmaster's initials), clamps, an apprentice's toolchest, and a store of tortoiseshell are identifiable among the many other items and paraphernalia necessary for the work of skilled craftsmen.

The antiques collector's father specialized in making church furniture, and today examples of his work, made from oak sourced locally, can be found in churches throughout west Oxfordshire. Within the workshop he constructed yew chairs destined for Oxford's Bodleian Library. The kitchen table, made from Italian walnut, was fashioned by him in Italy while recovering from injuries during World War II. The trestle-ended table measuring 7ft was shipped to England along with his naval stores. In an upstairs bedroom a walnut knee-hole desk is another creation treasured and used by his son and the rest of his family today.

On inheriting the house 15 years ago the antiques collector returned to his childhood home with his wife and children. His antiques business, specializing in furniture, glass, porcelain, and prints from the seventeenth to nineteenth centuries was already well-established. Commodities to be traded are sought locally from auctions, trade contacts, and private homes. Particular favourites are kept, and these comprise and complement the decorative fabric of the house, contributing to an eclectic aura of quality and history that is reflective of three successive generations' tastes and artistry.

The Clothes Importer

and the Clock House

Sometimes called The Clock House because of the eye-catching stable clock on its roof, this magical, historical building is part of a National Trust-owned property and estate, and home and workplace to an importer of Indian clothes and throws.

During the 1960s importing goods from foreign countries became a way of life for a woman with an eye for clean lines and simplicity. She became co-owner of Warehouse, a popular store in Covent Garden, London, which specialized in inexpensive objects, furniture, and clothes. In her quest for new merchandise she travelled to India, where the seeds of a deep-seated love for the country and its products were sown.

Initially she looked for rugs, bedspreads, toys, jute bags – anything that caught her eye as being popular with British shoppers – but gradually she began to absorb and emulate Indian fashions and style. She discarded tight, tailored clothes from her own wardrobe in favour of the freedom and comfort of Indian kaftans, pyjamas, loose shirts, and skirts. She was drawn to the subtle vegetable dyes, traditional Indian designs, and pure white-on-white embroidery.

left The kitchen was previously the washing room in the old laundry; a pipe leading into the top of the arch seals a flue used in the past as a means for steam to escape. The arched door leads into a larder cupboard.

above The pictures on the narrow landing are of Indian scenes painted by the importer's husband and friends. A clear, lemon-yellow colour brightens the walls. Doors echo original arched-shaped alcoves downstairs.

left The kitchen leads directly onto a paved area – once a grassed drying area for the laundry. Slate and stones salvaged from the main house are used for the garden table.

right The view looking south beneath a canopy of leaves within the lime avenue, planted in 1965. For the importer's bi-annual catalogue, friends and family are photographed modelling the clothes in the house and surrounding gardens.

When she met and married her husband, Michael Wickham, and joined him in his National Trust haven overlooking the Vale of the White Horse in the southern Cotswolds, the fabric importer took her business with her. Now her step-daughter and grandchildren live in one wing of the clock tower, and the importer shares her own "side" with many of her late husband's artistic legacies and paintings.

The house was originally the "laundry" of a much bigger building, sadly destroyed by fire in 1952, which stood on a plateau of lawn overlooking surrounding parkland. This land had degenerated into a weedy field until Michael created a garden there in 1989. Box-hedging cuttings were used to outline the ground-floor plan of the original house. He also planted a lime avenue in 1965 that now forms a well-canopied tunnel of dense overhead foliage in the summer.

Throughout the house a myriad of Indian materials cover sofas, beds, and cushions, frame windows, or are worn by day or night. Outside, in the old stable block, a "showroom" houses shirts, tops, waistcoats, dresses, jackets, kaftans, shawls, and throws – all characterized by their colourful individuality. Such was the thickness of the walls in the old washing room (now the kitchen) that a larder cupboard was made within the thickness of the original wall. Similarly dormer windows and bedroom cupboards were

created in the deep walls upstairs. Forty years ago, when only one National Trust agent managed the area from Coventry to the Isle of Wight, home-improvements of this nature were often overlooked and allowed to stay, and Michael's handiwork still gives pleasure today.

Underpinning the whole ethos of life in the clock tower is the free, unfitted, unconventional nature of Indian clothing. In a paved, walled garden leading directly from the kitchen, roses, acanthus, and the delicate white blooms of *crambe cordifolia* grow freely, and colourful annuals self-seed, unchecked among the cracks in paving stones. One end of the kitchen is devoted to gardening paraphernalia. In a world where open-plan living and clean-cut minimalism are prevalent, the effect is refreshingly idiosyncratic.

below Open brickwork is painted with hyacinth-blue powder paint. A gilt-framed mirror and a polished "tall boy" add an air of comfort and style.

right The double-height drawing room is decorated with Indian bedspreads and cushions, and eighteenth-century English clocks.

The Florist

and the Cow Shed

A florist and her family have made the outbuildings
of a Cotswold farmhouse into a light, airy home
where the overall style is simplistic and uncluttered,
surrounded by fields and the open countryside
of the Oxfordshire Cotswolds.

left A double-height drawing room fills a space previously occupied by a run of cow stalls. The hearth is a stone slab from the farmyard, the log basket an old mail basket on wheels, and large pebbles have become containers for lilies.

below right In the main bedroom a nineteenth-century American quilt, loved for its textures and faded colours, hangs behind the double bed. Fresh gingham checks are prevalent throughout the house.

overleaf The kitchen is spacious and light. Towels hang on a wooden A-shaped ecclesiastical hanger designed for clergy's gowns; rows of jugs double as containers for both milk and flowers.

Flowers have been central to the florist's life since, as a small child, she helped her mother create floral decorations for churches and cathedrals. Her father was a choir master and an organist, which led to an unusual childhood spent in and around cathedral closes. Now she runs a business providing flowers for weddings, private houses, and special occasions; but her strength lies not in formal, studied arrangements but in spontaneous, imaginative flourishes that celebrate the four seasons and her clients' personalities.

The florist is a firm believer in there being no right or wrong way to arrange flowers, just as long as fresh, seasonal, country ingredients are central to each design. Unusual containers – often practical servicable items such as graters, jugs, baskets, and enamel colanders – are part of this philosophy. Stems of blackberry bush bearing fruits of various ripeness, gathered from the hedgerow while out dog-walking, could ramble over the sides of a pudding basin in autumn, and berries and twigs of every description could be used to maximum effect in appropriate receptacles during the Christmas period. Using out-of-season produce at any time – such as strawberries or delphiniums at Christmas – is not the florist's style.

Within the house the lack of frivolous artifice is a constant characteristic. While the florist's love of flowers is expressed in floral fabrics, pictures, and in the presence of fresh flowers in every room, her love of foliage and its different textures is expressed in the ubiquitous green-and-cream colour schemes and the fresh simplicity of gingham squares and checks. Natural fibres and textures bathed in natural light are a frequent feature. The U-shaped kitchen, originally the farm's tractor shed, is an open, uncluttered space where the florist's love of cream-painted soft wood and her dislike of clinical tiles is evident. Heart motifs, a symbol of the Shaker philosophy "hands for work, hearts for God", are prevalent. Unconsciously the florist's work and her Cotswold lifestyle are fulfilling this creed in every way.

below An inner container within a cream-and-white colander holds a natural, seasonal arrangement of cabbages, white roses, purple thistles, and heather among green garden foliage.

right The florist collects English green and cream enamelware. The wooden floral-painted panel behind the sink was created by the florist's elder daughter as part of her school art exam.

The Equestrian
and the Farmhouse

A farmhouse has been painstakingly restored over
the last five years to become the Cotswold home of a
family of six. The twenty-four acres that come with
the house, and its central position for equestrian
events, makes it ideal for a family dedicated to horses.

left At the top of the landing
the bottom half of an
eighteenth-century dresser
supports a row of pewter
plates, beneath a print of
a horse that belonged to
the Prince of Wales in 1800.

right A view through the
English oak banisters of
the Jacobean staircase to the
outer and inner hallways via
a Farmington stone archway.
The staircase was made locally
to match an original design
at nearby Carswell Manor.

Horses have played a central role in a mother's life since she was three years old. Despite
non-horsey parents, she grew up 400 yards from a reputable riding school and such was her
enthusiasm and the diversity of her talent that, after competing at the prestigious
Badminton and Burghley horse trials aged 21 years, she became a flat jockey, racing at
Epsom, Ascot, and York. Following a break for four babies, during which she successfully
developed a livery and training business, she returned to flat racing and only hung up her
boots when one daughter's blossoming career began to absorb all her time.

Although all the family ride, or are remarkably successful in other sporting arenas, it is the
international eventing career of the eldest daughter that dictates the family's way of life.
She has already represented her country four times in European Championships, winning
three team silvers and one gold medal, and is realistically ambitious to represent her
country at the highest level. The cycle of preparation is relentless: January and February are
spent developing the horses' fitness for the event season of March to October. During the
winter 10 or 12 horses must be mucked out and 8 or 10 trained every day: "You can never
stop learning or teaching to achieve top results, and you are only as good as your last win."

The same creed underpins the father's methodical style of house restoration. The third
generation of his family to live in the Cotswolds, he sold a farm on the outskirts of Witney

left An Aga cooker plays a vital role, airing clothes and equipment and warming the horses' feed. New kitchen units made by local craftsmen were painted and distressed to look scuffed and worn in.

below left The back door, one of a pair from Provence, is made from medieval oak. Leather waterproof boots are considered an essential element of the family's equestrian wardrobe.

right An Elizabethan three-plank table stands at the foot of the Jacobean staircase; it shifts sideways in December to accommodate a tall Christmas tree. The pewter candle-holders are modelled on a sixteenth-century design.

left A young five-year-old bay gelding, an exciting prospect in the eventing world, relaxes at home in one of the 12 loose boxes.

right Double rows of saddle-racks in the tack room support an array of racing and general-purpose saddles and other vital equipment including girths, boots, and numnahs (saddle pads).

in favour of this rural farmhouse, with its acres of land. He had admired the house as a child and had watched, in dismay, as it had passed through hands unsympathetic to its indiginous Cotswold origins. He spent three years restoring it, using local materials (for example, Farmington stone for fireplaces and arches) and re-installing Cotswold characteristics such as stone-mullioned windows. Wood panelling was reinstated, aided by local craftsmen skilled in the art of distressing new work to look authentically old. Outside, the generous amount of land represented a blank equestrian canvas; now there are loose boxes, a horse walker, an all-weather school, and numerous post-and-railed paddocks.

In deference to the family's equestrian way of life, carpets have been dispensed with and flagstones laid throughout. A boot-room at the back of the house buffers the detritus that inevitably follows horses; a self-closing door seals it from the main house. The kitchen/breakfast/sitting room is the nucleus of the house, and an Aga cooker is a vital component not only for cooking family meals but for drying breeches, girths, and boots, and for the slow cooking necessary for the horses' feed of boiled barley and linseed. Despite the spaciousness of the house the family always gravitate to the kitchen, where their Cotswold life is often conducted alongside the repetitive "clunk" of metal girth buckles rotating in the washing machine.

Index

Acknowledgments

The author, photographer, and stylist would like to thank all the families and individuals featured in this book who have let us into their lives and their homes.
Some may be contacted directly, as follows:

The Cook – Email: emmaschuster@tiscali.co.uk

The Custodian – www.owlpen.com
Tel: 01453 860261

The Sculptress – Email: Lbaillie2704@aol.com

The Bookbinder – Tel: 01367 242768

The Knitwear Designer – Maggie White, Burford
Tel: 01993 822600 (shop)

The Carpenter – Tel: 01452 813433

The Clothes Importer – www.dennyandrews.co.uk

The Florist – Tel: 01993 878237

Finally, we dedicate this book to our spouses –
David, Jenny, and Nick – for their help and support.

All pictures are copyright of Mark Nicholson, 2004
www.marknicholson.com

To purchase limited-edition prints from the book and other associated products visit **www.englishcountryinteriors.com**

Further Reading

Gibbings, L.V. (ed), *The Cotswold Sheep*, Cotswold Sheep Society 1995

Hadfield, C. & A.M., *The Cotswolds: A New Study*, David & C 1973

Hill, Michael and Birch, Sally, *Cotswold Stone Homes*, Sutton Publishing 1998

Hollingsworth, Alan, *Cotswold Architecture and Heritage*, Grange Books 1992

Hollingsworth, Alan, *Cotswold Landscape*, Grange Books 1991

Jones, Anthea, *The Cotswolds*, Phillimore & Co. Ltd. 1994

Knowles, Christopher, *The Cotswolds*, AA Publishing 2002

Lewis, June, *The Cotswolds: Life and Traditions*, Weidenfeld & Nicholson Illustrated 1996

Moriarty, Denis, *Buildings of the Cotswolds*, Victor Gollancz 1989

Brooks, Alan and Verey, David, *Gloucestershire: The Cotswolds (Pevsner Buildings of England Series)*, Yale University Press 2002

Turner, Joanna, *Quarries and Craftsmen of the Windrush Valley*, Burford and District Society 1988

Herbert, N.M. (ed), *History of the County of Gloucester*, Victoria County History of the Counties of England 1981